IMAGINAIRE V
Contemporary Magic Realism

www.fantasmus.com

INTRODUCTION

Little news has happened since the latest IMAGINAIRE. The crises seems to keep a ferm grip on the world, though I have been told that it has not effected the BRIC countries, so perhaps this is a world to discover.
Phantasten Museum in Vienna is still making efforts to promote the fantastic art. This is very important as so little from official side are happening in Europe. We must hope they can stay as this bastion of an example for the rest of Europe.

*Hilleroed Librabry - Freak Show
Kasper Holten, NG Hammer,
Aleksander Kosmala, Siegfried Zademack,
Lukas Kandl, Peter van Oostzanen,
Tommas, Michael Hiep, Gert Brasque,
Claus Brusen, Dag Samsund
and fan No.1 – Oliver!*

Viechtach, in the Bavarian mountains in Germany, also have made a centre for the fantastic art so things are moving along and we shall one day be more visible on the general art scene.

Apart from a load of fine exhibitions done by the Phantasten Museum in Vienna in the past year, we, in FANTASMUS, have also had some exhibitions. December 2011 + 2012, an erotic show for artists in IMAGINAIRE, March - May 2012 a larger group show at Hilleroed Library, again mainly participants in IMAGINAIRE and last here in October 2012, just before the deadline of IMAGINAIRE 5, a group show in Helsinge, DK. So within a year Fantasmus has done no less than 4 exhibitions, despite the crises.
We cannot give up the fight, even though money may be small, we still have to do whatever we can to maintain our position in the art world of today.

It seems that Facebook is the new site to use for promoting and inviting. Within the past 2 years most activity is going on there which I find good as you get instant feedback directly instead of a fine homepage. Not to say homepages are not needed anymore. They are still very valuable as a sort of CV of the artists.

I have not been presented to many new art books in the past year. This of course also because of the crises. The team of FANTASMUS released a book by and about our designer, Bruno, in October 2012. This book is more a picture book with examples of his long career as a freelance illustrator, showing his many jobs given by companies and private people. Furthermore his own art is shown here. All with his great sense of humour. The text is just written only in Danish.

Another great book I was pleased to be given is the book on the work of Paul Raymond Gregory, "Beyond Time and Place". A beautiful book from this brilliant painter with a full display of his career as an artist for Heavy Metal artwork like Saxon, Dio and Molly Hackett - just to mention a few. Along with those, more commercial pieces, it also contains Paul's passion for Lord of the Rings, a display of museum pieces, large and beautiful paintings from his career through more than 30 years. All Tolkien paintings are framed individually to match the story in the paintings, which gives a fabulous symbioses. We are working on bringing a larger solo exhibition with Paul's work to Denmark.

*Phantasten Museum, Vienna
Kate Eggleston-Wirtz, Eike Erzmoneit, Claus Brusen, Brigid Marlin, Michel De Saint Ouen, Ernst Fuchs, Erich Peischl, Gerhard Habarta and Ernst Steiner*

Galeria in Bedskidska, Poland will again in 2013 make a great big group show. This is planned to take place in September. The second time they arrange a larger international group show. The first exhibition was also shown in Italy. Poland now is on the list of countries where things are happening.

Tim Roosen and NovaBelgica in Belgium unfortunately had to stop their activities as a center in Belgium, mainly as in so many cases because of lack of funds and in some cases lack of professionalism from some artists. I cannot blame any artists for having difficulties during this crises, but it is unfair to let down those few who, despite the crises, try to arrange lager events, spending time and money to put something together and artists saying yes to participate and then you never hear from them again even though they are on posters and invitations. It is fair enough to say; "Sorry, I cannot participate as I have no money to ship artwork, please don't forget me next time!!!"
We can all be in a situation like this.

These are the words from the editor
for this the fifth edition of IMAGINAIRE.

Claus Brusen Dec. 2012.

IMAGINAIRE V   5

Greetings from the new partner in
FANTASMUS

Having had the pleasure of being invited to exhibitions, having travelled to international shows with Claus Brusen etc. made by FANTASMUS through some years, it became more and more to my knowledge that I wanted to make a personal effort for both FANTASMUS and fantastic art. In June 2012 the decission was made and I became equally partner in FANTASMUS. We reestablished the company in England in June 2012 and along with that we made our department in Denmark.

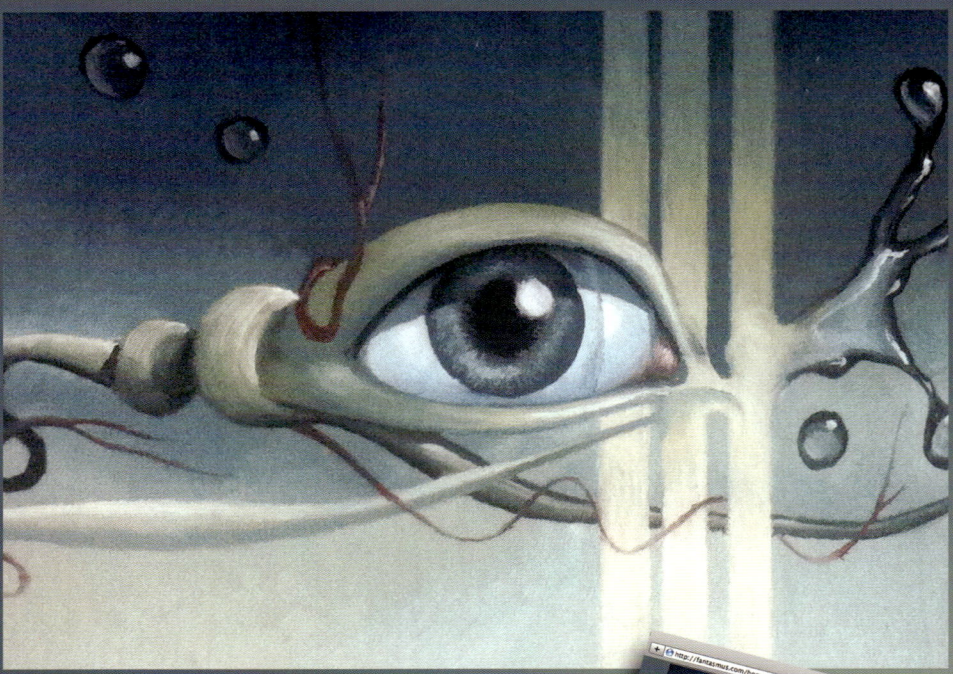

Claus Brusen · The Eye
Oil on panel 1995 (detail)

Since then several exiting things has happened. We have launched our new webpage – www.fantasmus.com - and along with that a new logo for FANTASMUS. The site is still under construction but keeps growing steady every week. The service of making webpages is yet another thing FANTASMUS can offer for artists and all others interested. Still it is of course a possility for interested artists to have books both designed, printed, published, sold and distributed through FANTASMUS.

During fall 2012 we moved the company to new locations just north of Copenhagen. Here we are able to do all work and furthermore also have smaller exhibitions. So far we have had the usual "Erotic Christmas" and that was a great success. The vernissage was on December 1st and many artists from both Denmark and Europe attended both with art and personally. Thank you all for the massive back up you have shown us!

Curating a group show in October in Helsinge Kulturhus north of Copenhagen we had the pleasure of showing no less than 21 international and of course Danish artist and more than 70 pieces of art. A very succesfull and large exhibition with a great, positive response from a massive amount of people.

In the beginning of November we made a small visit in England where we had the pleasure of attending Paul Gregory's book launch at O2. That led us to a talk with Paul about showing his album covers in an exhibition in Denmark. We are working on that in this writing moment. We also had the pleasure of spending time with Mark and Julie Wilkinson with whom we plan our huge project 12 painters – 12 Musicians titled "FANTASMUS – FANTAStic art and MUSic". The great honor of having met Anthony Phillips, who is also taking part of the project, came along while being in England. My greatest respect hereby send to the three of you showing your trust is us and our project!!! Worth mentioning is that we hope to cooperate with "Save the Children" worldwide so that the profit will benefit children in need.

Julie and Mark Wilkinson
www.the-masque.com

Erotic Christmas 2012
Helle Rask Crawford

Phantasten Museum, Vienna
Ernst Fuchs and
Mette Torp Bisgaard

Spring and summer 2013 already have a list of wonderful projects. 1st of all the launch of IMAGINAIRE V. Thank you David M. Bowers for your eye cathing painting for our book cover. During easter we aim to have a solo exhibition at FANTASMUS for Claus Brusen. In the beginning of June the next exhibition called "LOVE" will take place also at our own location. This will be a miniature show with a maximum size for paintings of A5. And then of course during fall another IMAGINAIRE will be published. The guest of honour in the next edition will be Micha Lobi and we are so much looking forward to that.

I would very much like to thank especially Tegner Bruno for his merciful patience with us during the whole process of making the book. And thanks to all artists for attending yet another beautiful art book. And of course a huge thanks to my partner Claus Brusen for having put up with me as a new apprentice!

I am happy taking part of this wonderful world and am so much looking forward to many great and exiting projects, happenings etc. in many years to come.

Enjoy the book and please keep updated on FANTASMUS

Co-owner of FANTASMUS

Mette Torp Bisgaard

Not just dreams, but goals for the future of
FANTASMUS

Claus Brusen
Campanula Concerto, Opus 122
Oil on panel · 2004

In the future the ultimate dream is to establish a museum, and a foundation along with it, in Scandinavia to honor and exhibit a variety of artists from all over the world. FANTASMUS will of course be the name for it – FANTAStic MUSeum. This to make a tribute to the genre Imaginary Realism as it needs and deserves a place of its own in our part of the world. A very special collection of 30 * 30 cm paintings has already been started. We aim to get a large collection to make a beatiful frieze at the museum. For all interested artist our request is for you to donate a painting in this size to be put into the foundation and then be permanently displayed at the museum. Apart from paintings shown here the collection also contains paintings from Patrick Woodroffe, Wolfgang Harms, Michael Parkes etc.

We can do it – If you want it!!!!!

By coincidence we were fortunate enough to get to know an artist from another part of the artistic scene. Namely an opera singer from The Royal Danish Opera – Søren Aagaard. He has made an old and huge wish come true introducing us to The Royal Theatre from the inside. Hopefully the Symphony Orchestra finds it interesting having Claus Brusen making a huge painting of them all with their instruments in his world "Nactalius". Along with that I will write the story of the orchestra and also the story of each instrument individually. This is a project which will be going on for a couple of years and is supposed to end up with both the large painting, smaller paintings and sketches and a book about both the orchestra and the whole process of it all including of course both photos and paintings to accompany the text.

Having gotten involved in FANTASMUS has payed off more than just work and great experiences. The business and all that comes along with it is not just 40 hours of work a week. It is 24/7/365. And how can we do that without getting to know each other very well? The answer is simply – we can't! Our relationship has evolved and is not just a partnership in business but also in private. On June 5th 2013 Claus and I will get married and as we are fortunate enough to have lots of both Danish and International artists attending along with, of course, our family and friends. We hereby announce that the Miniature Show about love of course is because of our wedding. The vernissage will be close to the wedding so that all artists attending our wedding can be present in person at the vernissage.

Back us up in our efforts to make it happen

Mette Torp Bisgaard

Michael Hiep · The Nightmare of the White Widdow · 30 x 30 cm · Oil on panel

David Stoupakis · Enemy of one · 30 x 30 cm · Oil on panel

Linda Groen · We love him · 30 x 30 cm · Oil on canvas

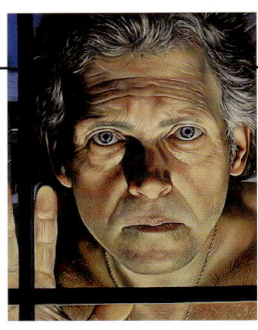

DAVID M. BOWERS
1956 USA
www.dmbowers.com

The Wish · 30,5 x 30,5 cm · Oil on panel

Artificial Love · 45 x 60 cm · Oil on linen

The Ham · 35 x 35 cm · Oil on wood

DAVID MICHAEL BOWERS' OBSERVATIONS
FOREWORD BY THE ARTIST

The Messenger · 76 x 101,5 cm · Oil on linen

I am often asked by reporters, collectors, and people in general where the ideas for my paintings come from. My answer is that all artists are observers of the culture and society in which they live. It doesn't matter in what age the artist lives. I believe human nature is the same throughout the ages. The names, clothing, and locations change, but human nature, for better or worse, is largely predictable, and has been for the last 5,000 years.

We all then are observers of the human parade. Voyeurers who try to understand the triumphs and failures of humanity. All human beings ask the same questions about our existence, "Why do we act the way we do?" Are we alone in the universe? Are we missing important knowledge about our past?"

One thing that complicates our observations of human nature is the gaps in our own history. Many scientists, including archeologists and anthropologists, strive to fill in theses holes in our history. Unfortunately, scientists often find more questions than answers.

Our species sadly has been controlled by superstition and primal reactions instead of reason. One only has to look at the Middle East where humans have been killing each other for 2,000 years over three religions that may all be the result of contact with alien visitors and unidentified flying objects.

Hundreds of tribal histories, religions, and ancient books tell of visitors from the stars who impart knowledge to humans and then leave. Is this the basis of our major religions?

I am fascinated by observing human beings and their place in the universe. The fact that tens of thousands of credible witnesses believe that the earth is being visited by alien life forms brings up countless questions.

Fantasy artists, like all free thinking people, have explored these questions that these legends recount. Art, should above all, stimulate the senses and promote intellectual discussion. Far too many people abdicate their participation in solving the questions about our very origins and existence. They blindly follow power structures, like governments and religion, to avoid thinking about uncomfortable ideas.

These disquieting ideas are important to Fantasy Artists. It is a safe bet that given the size of the universe, with billions of planets, that anything we can imagine probably exists somewhere in the cosmos.

Science fiction writers and Fantasy Artists are often decades ahead of science and technology. What is important about this fact is that their work may act as the inspiration for advances in science, new inventions, and historical research.

My art explores human interaction and how individuals react to the power structures that control our lives. What compromises do people make to survive in an increasingly complex and interlocking world?

The age old difference between men and women and their perceptions of the world are favorite topics in my work. How women use their intelligence, sexuality and social poise in their constant jockeying with men, has often entered my paintings.

The fact that I have collectors all over the world has always pleased me, and that my paintings cross cultural and international boundaries is also exciting. I believe art should reach out to all people and stimulate thinking and the search for truth. Only when reason replaces superstition and primal reactions will humans solve many of the Earth's problems.

As time goes by, and I see myself aging, I begin to think of my own mortality. Several of my recent paintings indicate my thought processes. Family Tree and The Observer are self portraits that reflect my continuing self analysis.

All artists wonder if their work will stand the test of time. What will future generations think of David Michael Bowers? Will my paintings find their way from private collections to museums? I have seen that many good artists and their works have been relegated to obscurity and this has always depressed me. They are the victims of fads and fancy as taste and interests continually change and evolve. There are talented artists who have lived in the past and are relatively unknown except to a few scholars and
serious collectors. Their work may rival some of the artists whose names are household words. Why then did they not gain fame? Is it bad luck or the lack of agents to promote them? Perhaps their work did not find its way into important collections or museums. These are some of the frustrating questions that complicate the lives of all artists.

One must rely on an inner strength and have faith in ones own talents. Artists must believe in their own vision and hope that just a portion of the population shares their views.

I am honored to be highlighted in this book with the works of so many excellent artists. Claus Brusen has searched the world for those whose work has something special to convey to the people of planet Earth.

The Observer · 73,5 x 45,5 cm · Oil on panel

Happy Days Are Here Again · 40 x 51 cm · Oil on panel

Rudolf · 91,5 x 101,5 cm · Oil on linen

14 IMAGINAIRE V

Access Denied · 43 x 35,5 cm · Oil on panel

Suburban Taboo · 40 x 60 cm · Oil on linen

The Ice Princess · 65 x 48 cm · Oil on panel

The Three Graces · 61 x 56 cm · Oil on linen

Quest for Immortality · 35,5 x 28 cm · Oil on linen

The Crown · 86 x 51 cm · Oil on linen

The Eternal Touch · 122 x 86,3 cm · Oil on linen

Fanatsy Friend · 35,5 x 56 cm · Oil on panel

The Unresponsive Audience · 122 x 91,5 cm · Oil on linen

Safe Sex · 122 x 91,5 cm · Oil on linen

It's Coming · 66 x 40,6 cm · Oil on linen mounted to panel

Sister's Secrets · 45,7 x 35,5 cm · Oil on linen

The Tool Man · 50,8 x 40,6 cm · Oil on panel

Veg-Head · 40,6 x 35,5 cm · Oil on panel

Pig Walker II · 63,5 x 48,2 cm · Oil on panel

ALAYNE ABRAHAMS
USA 1953
www.alayneabrahams.com

Shadow Box · 70 x 50 cm · Mixed media of watercolor and colored pencil

Moondancer · 70 x 50 cm · Watercolor

CLAUS BRUSEN
1960 Denmark
www.clausbrusen.com

Odd couple · Round 31 cm · Oil on panel

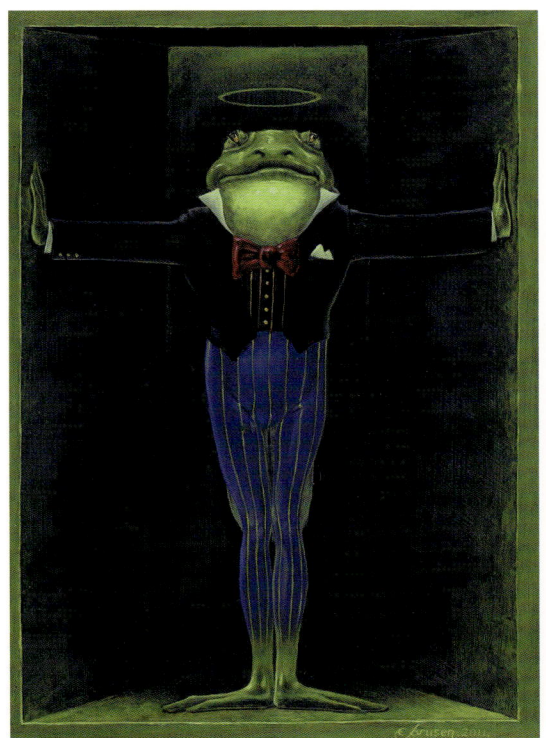
Frog in a box · 17,8 x 12,5 cm · Oil on panel

Mr. Nice Mouse · 17,8 x 12,5 cm· Oil on panel

Sir. Owl · 17,8 x 12,5 cm · Oil on panel

Strugle · 17,8 x 12,5 cm· Oil on panel

The little Prince and his true Guard · 30,1 x 23,6 cm · Oil on panel

Pinappelis Musicanta · 27 x 22 cm · Oil on panel

GIL BRUVEL
1959 USA
www.bruvel.com

In an intimate emotional connection, where does the boundary lie between inside and outside, between me and you? Like a twisting Möbius strip that forms an infinite loop, the powerful flow of energy within and between us moves freely, unconstrained by such notions as skin or space or time.

Never Ending conveys this visceral sense of seamlessness, while also honoring the parallel currents that make up two distinct yet intertwined lives. Bruvel's evocative sculpture also hints that memories or feelings, like bubbles in the stream of time, may sometimes gather – as on the female figure's chest – and sometimes remain dispersed. And what of the eyes – his like open windows, hers intently fixed? One imagines that in a different moment, her eyes instead would allow his steady gaze to flow straight through.

As the artist puts it: "It makes sense that we look through each other to see ourselves." Yet the answers to every question stirred up by the work may be as fluid as the piece itself. When viewed from various angles, the figures present entirely different aspects of their relationship – all existing simultaneously, all changing with the flow of time, and each one true.

Never Ending · 76 x 61 x 94 cm · Stainless Steel

Rain · 51 x 43 x 35,5 cm · Stainless Steel

HELLE RASK CRAWFORD
1964 Denmark
www.helleraskcrawford.dk

Borderlands · 35 x 62 x 25 cm · Bronze

The steadfast Tin Soldier · 25 x 20 x 10 cm · Bronze

Of Aurochs and Angels · 35 x 62 x 25 cm · Bronze

VAL DYSHLOV
1950 USA
www.valdyshlov.com

Reality · 69 x 89 cm · Oil on canvas

In one's sleep · 28 x 36 cm · Oil on canvas

Birthday · 30 x 30 cm · Oil on canvas

After Evana Kupala · 92 x 122 cm · Oil on canvas

Flight above Desert · 92 x 122 cm · Oil on canvas

IMAGINAIRE V

IGOR GRECHANYK
1960 Ukraine
www.grechanyk.com

Touch of Imagination · 75 cm H · Bronze

Touch of Imagination (fragment) · 75 cm H · Bronze

STEPHANIE HENDERSON
1959 USA
www.hendersonart.com

The Blind Man · 130 x 90 cm · Mixed media

Underwater in Outer Space · 78,5 x 91,5 cm · Oil on linen

The big BANG · 86,3 x 170 cm · Oil on linen

MICHAEL HIEP
1959 The Netherlands
www.michaelhiep.nl

The growing-up of the Mermaid · 70 x 50 cm · Oil on panel

My Muse · 90 x 60 cm · Oil on panel

STEVEN KENNY
1962 USA
www.stevenkenny.com

Bubbles · 71 x 91 cm · Oil on canvas

The Surrender · 66 x 66 cm · Oil on canvas

RICHARD A. KIRK
1962 Canada
www.richardakirk.com

Peering into Darkness · 25 x 30 cm · Ink on paper

Dustmill · 22 x 30 cm · Ink on paper

Insomnia · 55 x 35 cm · Ink on paper

Chimera · 112 x 87 cm · Ink on paper

Out of a Violent Planet · 40 x 30 cm · Ink on paper

Harrowing Sediment · 75 x 55 cm · Ink on paper

PATRICK VAN DER LINDE

1972 The Netherlands
www.patrickvanderlinde.nl

Dead End · 45 x 80 cm · Oil on canvas

High Light · 16 x 12 cm · Oil on panel

In the clouds · 12 x 16 cm · Oil on panel

Ruin with Church Door · 16 x 12 cm · Oil on panel

THOR LINDENEG

1941 Denmark
www.lindeneg.dk

Accessories · 75 x 60 cm · Oil on canvas

Duet · 95 x 75 cm · Oil on canvas

Ot2 · 70 x 50 cm · Oil on canvas

Smile · 40 x 33 cm · Oil on canvas

JACK LIPOWCZAN

1951 Poland/Germany

www.jali-art.com

Woman in Red or Polish Bucolica · 95 x 115 cm · Oil on panel

High Society or the Luncheon on the Grass · 70 x 95 cm · Oil on panel

European Madonnas - Polonia · 95 x 70 cm · Oil on panel   European Madonnas - Germania · 95 x 70 cm · Oil on panel   European Madonnas - Helvetia · 95 x 70 cm · Oil on panel

Marriage of Convenience · 50 x 65 cm · Oil on panel

Captain's War · 50 x 65 cm · Oil on panel

Into Magical Dreams · 70 x 95 cm · Oil on panel

Unexpected Pilgrimage or surprise Visit · 70 x 95 cm · Oil on panel

With a Friendly Help for Brussels · 50 x 65 cm · Oil on panel

MICHA LOBI
1967 Sibiria
www.fantasmus-art.com • m.lobi@mail.ru

Nightshift · 24,5 x 38 cm · Tempera/oil on panel

Christmas Marked · 40 x 49 cm · Tempera/oil on panel

Holiday · 25 x 50 cm · Tempera/oil on panel

Moonlight · 18 x 38 cm · Tempera/oil on panel

Aprilsündrin · 51 x 62 cm · Tempera/oil on panel

LUDMILA
1958 Russia / Portugal
www.ludmila-fantasticart.blogspot.com

Minotauro · 50,5 x 57 cm · Oil on board

Accidental Kiss · 125 x 100 cm · Oil on board

BRIGID MARLIN
UK
www.brigidmarlin.com

The Rose Garden · 46 x 38 cm · Mische technique

The Golden Cord · 48 x 92 cm · Mische technique

Girl in Bluebell Wood · 56 x 70 cm · Mische technique

IMAGINAIRE V

CHRISTINE MORREN

1966 Belgium

www.christinemorren.com

The old Doll can't feed the Bird · 35 x 27 cm · Oil on wood

She bought a Pet · 35 x 27 cm · Oil on wood

AUTUMN SKYE MORRISON

1983 Canada

www.autumnskyemorrison.com

I aim to share honesty and awakening. To celebrate this fantastic adventure.
To inspire and be inspired.
May my paintings be a mirror, a reflection of our universal light, our human essence, and our timeless divinity.

Communion · 76 x 76 cm · Acrylic on canvas

Divinity Rising · 91,5 x 30,5 cm · Acrylic on canvas

The Guardian · 18 x 12,5 cm · Graphite and acrylic on paper

Wisdom of the Ages · 101,5 x 66 cm · Acrylic on canvas

PETER VAN OOSTZANEN

1962 The Netherlands

www.vanoostzanen.com

Dead Sparrow · 30 x 40 cm · Oil on panel

Desiree · 80 x 120 cm · Oil on canvas

Goudvis Syndicate · 60 x 80 cm · Oil on panel

IMAGINAIRE V

DANIELA OVTCHAROV
1964 Bulgaria / USA
www.ovtcharovart.com

Summer Night Flowers · 81 x 117 cm · Oil on canvas

The Graces · 117 x 168 cm · Oil on canvas

Fairy Land · 109 x 140 cm · Oil on canvas

The Flight · 117 x 168 cm · Oil on canvas

VLADIMIR OVTCHAROV
1963 Bulgaria / USA
www.ovtcharovart.com

The Mill and the Wheel · 106 x 76 cm · Acrylic on canvas

Beautiful Mind · 106 x 76 cm · Acrylic and pencil on canvas

GRASZKA PAULSKA

Poland
www.grazapp.deviantart.com

70 x 100 cm · Pastel on Canson paper

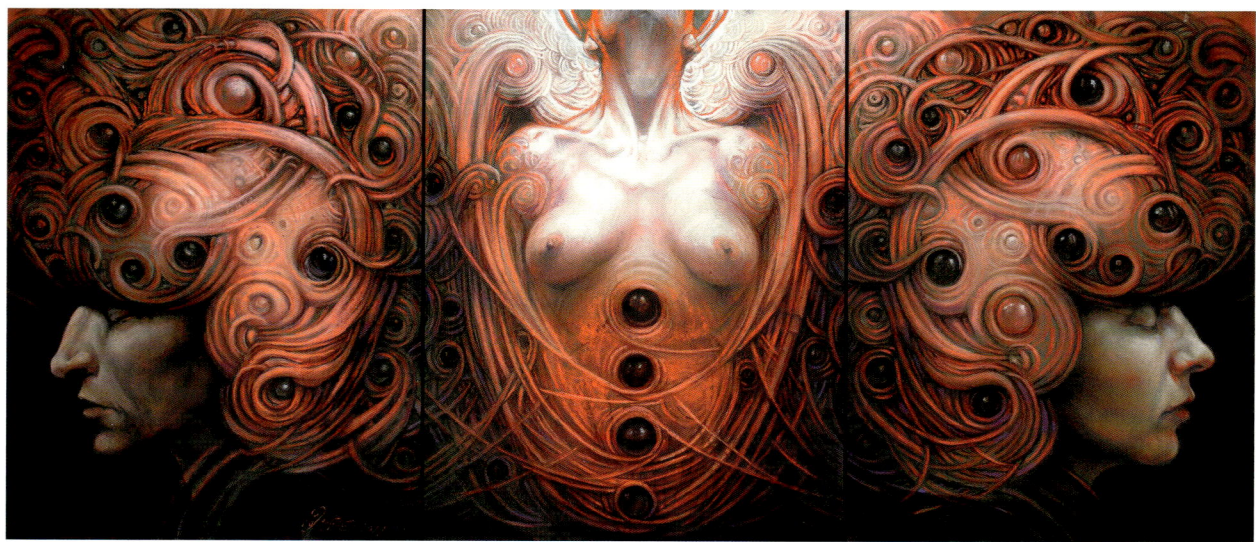

Triptych · 65 x 150 cm (3 x 65 x 50 cm) · Pastel on Canson paper

I'm in the Shadow of You · 100 x 60 cm · Oil

ISABELLE PLANTÉ
1949 France
www.isabelleplante.com

Le Cercle de Jeu · 65 x 54 cm · Oil on canvas

Les Bonnes Nouvelles · 55 x 46 cm · Oil on canvas

La Quintessence · 65 x 81 cm · Oil on canvas

TIM ROOSEN

1972 Belgium

www.timroosen.be

Baskabas · Lifesize · Steel, copper and brass

Photos by
Ansgar Noeth
and Iris Bitter
www.ansgarnoeth.de

Belladonna · Lifesize · Steel, copper and wrought iron,

DAG SAMSUND
1949 Denmark
www.art-samsund.dk

Txt · 80 x 80 cm · Oil on panel

Freaks in the Circus Paranoia · 57 x 69 cm · Oil and tempera on panel

Freaks in the old Theater · 49 x 45 cm · Oil and tempera on panel

MICHAEL SASSERSON
1964 Denmark
www.sasserson.dk

Elde · 200 x 160 cm · Marsh Oak and Alabaster

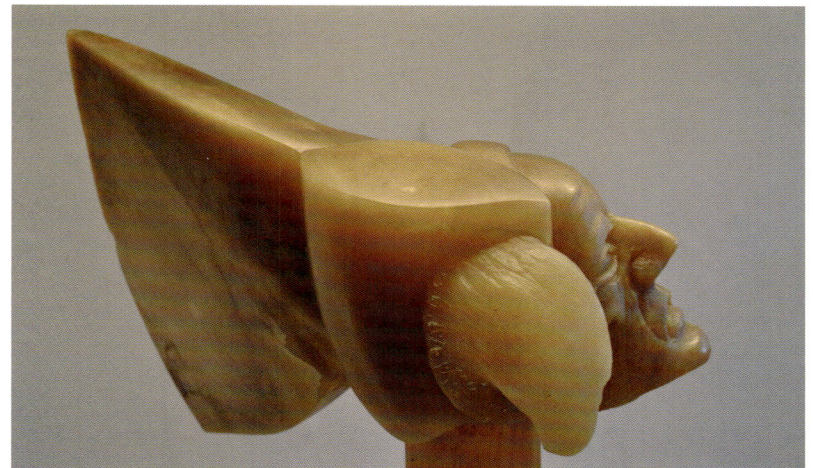

The last Mohican · 120 x 40 cm · Alabaster and Red Alder

Capitalism eats Mother Earth · 35 x 20 cm · Bronze and Clay

ISKREN SEMKOV
1984 Bulgaria
www.iskrensemkov.com

Unlock the Secret · 22 x 18 cm · Oil on canvas

Sea Memory · 40 x 40 cm · Oil on canvas

Metamórphosis · 10 x 10 cm · Oil on hardboard

Metamórphosis · 10 x 10 cm · Oil on hardboard

Transfiguration · 50 x 50 cm · Oil on canvas

Metamórphosis · 10 x 10 cm · Oil on hardboard

Tangerine Dream · 40 x 40 cm · Oil on canvas

IMAGINAIRE V **89**

JEAN THOMASSEN
1949 The Netherlands
www.jeanthomassen.nl

Last Judgment Day · 100 x 240 cm · Oil on panel

Last Judgment Day - Detail

A tribute to Maiu Blumberg · 100 x 80 cm · Oil on canvas

Portrait of Eva Maria · 90 x 70 cm · Oil on canvas

Portrait of Catharina · 90 x 70 cm · Oil on canvas

Cornelia Versluis, the artists mother, painted in a portrait from 1884 by Alfred Stevens · 51 x 41 cm · Oil on canvas

TWEEKUNST
Anne-Fieke & Eugène Later
1967 The Netherlands
www.tweekunst.nl

Message from the West · 58,5 x 102,5 cm · Oil on panel

The Tobias Symphony · 56,5 x 75 cm · Oil on panel

CLAUDE VERLINDE
1927 France
www.claude-verlinde.fr

La Danse Macabree · 91 x 63 cm · Oil on canvas stuck on panel

L instant · 60 x 120 cm · Oil on canvas stuck on panel

La Jetee · 125 x 146 cm · Oil on canvas stuck on panel

CAS WATERMAN
1958 The Netherlands
www.caswaterman.com

Hagazussa III · 30 x 20 cm · Oil on panel

Hagazussa II · 40 x 20 cm · Oil on panel

MARK WILKINSON
1952 England
www.the-masque.com

The Fool · 45,7 x 91,4 cm · Acrylic paint and airbrush acrylic ink on canvas

Return to Childhood · 45,7 x 91,4 cm · Acrylic paint and airbrush acrylic ink on canvas

PATRICK WOODROFFE
1940 England
www.patrickwoodroffe-world.com

"Brian Stewart" is happy and a Kiss from the real God · Round 30 cm · Oil on panel

The Start of the World and the Future · 63,4 x 40,6 cm · Oil on panel

SIEGFRIED ZADEMACK
1952 Germany
www.zademack.com

The Path of the Guardian Angel · 100 x 140 cm · Oil on linen

Dividing Line · 70 x 40 cm · Oil on linen

IMAGINAIRE V

Contemporary Magic Realism

First published in Denmark 2013
Copyright © 2013 Edition Brusen - FANTASMUS Artbooks

First edition

All rights reserved to the publisher. No part of this book may be reproduced or transmitted in any form, mannor or media including photography, recording or any other information storage and retrieval system, nor may pages be applied to any materials, cut, trimmed or sized to alter the excisting trim sizes (or) matted or framed with the intent to create other products for sale or resale or profit in any manor whatsoever, without prior permission in writing from the publisher or the artists.

IMAGINAIRE V.
2013, with reg.
ISBN: 978-87-993936-4-0
EAN: 9788799393640
ISSN: 1903-7708

Introduction by Claus Brusen

Special thanks to David M. Bowers and Mette Torp Bisgaard

Set in Garamond Premier Pro
Design and Layout by Tegner Bruno, Aalborg, Denmark
Prepress and Printing by Prinfo Aalborg, Denmark

Cover: David M. Bowers, The Pig Walker. Oil on wood
Inside cover Micha Lobi, Aprilsündrin. Tempera/oil on panel
Backside: A mix of whats inside

Distributed in Europe by Gazelle Book Service, UK   Distributed in North America by Independent Publisher Group

www.fantasmus.com

FANTASMUS ARTBOOKS PRESENTS

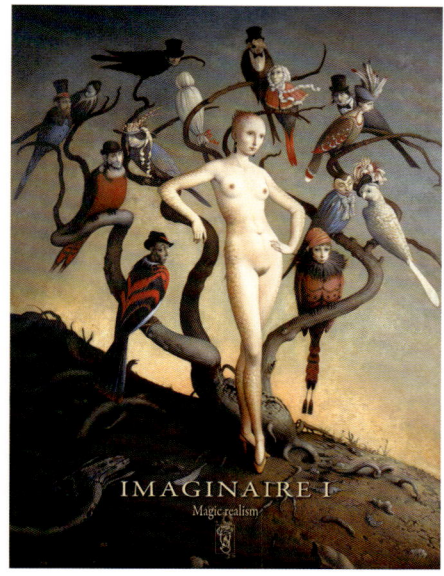

Imaginaire I
Hardcover · 31 x 22,5 cm · 148 pages
Released October 2008

Imaginaire II
Hardcover · 31 x 22,5 cm · 172 pages
Released September 2010

Imaginaire III
Hardcover · 31 x 22,5 cm · 200 pages
Released October 2011

Imaginaire IV
Hardcover · 31 x 22,5 cm · 168 pages
Released November 2011

Imaginaire V
Hardcover · 31 x 22,5 cm · 112 pages
Released February 2013

Imaginaire VI
Hardcover · 31 x 22,5 cm · 176 pages
Release date autumn 2013

Check at www.fantasmus.com to keep yourself updated

INDEX

Page 4
INTRODUCTION

Page 10
DAVID M. BOWERS

Page 28
ALAYNE ABRAHAMS

Page 30
CLAUS BRUSEN

Page 34
GIL BRUVEL

Page 36
HELLE RASK CRAWFORD

Page 38
VAL DYSHLOV

Page 40
IGOR GRECHANYK

Page 42
STEPHANIE HENDERSON

Page 44
MICHAEL HIEP

Page 46
STEVEN KENNY

Page 48
RICHARD A. KIRK

Page 52
PATRICK VAN DER LINDE

Page 54
THOR LINDENEG

Page 56
JACK LIPOWCZAN

Page 60
MICHA LOBI

Page 64
LUDMILA

Page 66
BRIGID MARLIN

Page 68
CHIRSTINE MORREN

Page 70
AUTUMN SKYE MORRISON

Page 72
PETER VAN OOSTZANEN

Page 74
DANIELA OVTCHAROV

Page 76
VLADIMIR OVTCHAROV

Page 78
GRASZKA PAULSKA

Page 80
ISABELLE PLANTÉ

Page 82
TIM ROOSEN

Page 84
DAG SAMSUND

Page 86
MICHAEL SASSERSON

Page 88
ISKREN SEMKOV

Page 90
JEAN THOMASSEN

Page 96
TWEEKUNST

Page 98
CLAUDE VERLINDE

Page 100
CAS WATERMAN

Page 102
MARK WILKINSON

Page 106
PATRICK WOODROFFE

Page 108
SIEGFRIED ZADEMACK